A CHILD'S HAPPY HEART

by Susan D. Amundson

illustrated by Brenda Joy Geiken

Susan Amundson
2001

Beaver's Pond Press, Inc.
Edina, Minnesota

ISBN 1-931646-08-2

Library of Congress Catalog Number: 2001093215

Printed in the United States of America.

05 04 03 02 01   6 5 4 3 2 1

Beaver's Pond Press, Inc.

5125 Danen's Drive
Edina, MN 55439-1465
(952) 829-8818
www.beaverspondpress.com
or
(651) 437-8244
toysammy@msn.com

PREFACE

With busy lifestyles in today's world children can sometimes, unintentionally, be put out to pasture.

When you study a bamboo tree you learn the primary years of its growth are working underground. All unseen parts are revealed later when it reaches above ground. At this time, the work that is done in the beginning surfaces.

A child's growth is very similar. Both root systems need a bundle of nurturing in the early years to grow strong and healthy.

We are all role models who can work together to prevent the scarring of a child's absorbent heart, and always remember:

> The birth of a child gives them the right to live and grow in the innocent stage of life known as childhood. This indisputable right should never be challenged by any force stronger than themselves.
>
> Susan D. Amundson, July 2001

This book and all subsequent Khobi and Hero books are dedicated to every child in our society.

MY SINCERE THANKS TO:

Illustrator, Brenda Geiken. Your gifted artwork of child innocence brings my story to life.

My family, for all your genuine infinite support of this project.

Mom and Dad, for your everlasting rays of sunshine.

My colleagues at school and friends who have kept the light burning.

My mentor, Milt Adams, for sharing years of experience.

And without question, the most precious resource. . . OUR BEAUTIFUL CHILDREN.

A CHILD'S HAPPY HEART

This is a story about a little Eskimo boy
named Khobi (descendant of
the ancient Samoyede people) and
his best friend, a Samoyed dog named
Bjelkiersam HERO®.
For reading ease Bjelkiersam HERO®
will be called Hero.

Khobi's journey begins. He leaves his Arctic homeland, lifted and blown south by the winds, to a commercialized city.

Whoa, Whoa, Whoaaaaaaaaaaaaaaaaaaaaaaaaaa, Swhee, Swhee, Swheeeeeeeeeeeeee . . . . strong gusts whirl and swirl Khobi and Hero into our world.

"Here we are Hero," Khobi tells his best friend, skidding his feet on the ground. "Whooooh, what a ride!"

In rolls Hero, resembling a squished cotton ball. With one quick shake from head to tail his coat stands out like someone has brushed him for hours. He looks magnificent and "HE" knows that too!

Khobi looks around and sees a modern day city. Big people are scurrying every which way. Dressed in snow-covered pelt clothing, with his co-mate alongside, two outsiders enter a new world together.

"Hero, look at all these frantic people. They don't even take the time to notice us. That tells me we have work to do here."

"Whuff, Whuff, Whuuuuuuuuuuurrrrrrrrrrrrfff," barks Hero, accepting his Alpha's observation.

Khobi was right. The grown-ups didn't even see this darling little boy and his beautiful fluffy pal.

When they attempt to cross the street, a driver of a cab shouts and beeps his horn many, many times. "Honk, Honk, Hooooooooooonk. Beep, Beep, Beeeeeeeeeep."

Stunned, Hero jumps back. His puffy tail drops down and does not wag. Two erect ears lay back and appear pasted to fur that is standing up with fright. Then he barks an answer "Whuff, Whuff, Whuuuuurrrrrrrrrrrrrrf (I think we're lost)."

Khobi gasps. They both recover from that noisy experience. Strength comes from each other. Taking a deep breath……… a sturdy little boy with his faithful companion continue on their way.

Now Khobi notices the stop and go lights. He learns quickly what they mean. "Maybe that's why that angry man honked at us," he tells Hero. "Red and green… looks like it means Stop and Go," learning this new lesson after he observes pedestrians. Khobi is a very smart little boy.

The young Northerners come by a schoolhouse. Seeing three children, they stop to share greetings.

"Hi, my name is Khobi. This is Hero." Khobi's eyes sparkle. Hero's tail wags as he bathes the children with doggy kisses. Smiles appear after receiving wet hellos.

"He wants to be your friend. That's a dog's way of saying 'I like you,'" educates Khobi.

"You're beautiful!" giggled a playful child being introduced to Hero's face washes. "Oh, hi! My name's Linda."

"They call me Joey."

"And I'm Susie."

All three children have now introduced themselves to this Arctic duo.

"Where did he come from?" they ask, while hugging the fluff–ball, burying their cold cheeks into his warm downy fur.

"Hero and I are from the far far northern part of the world. We live where it's very cold," Khobi tells the curious youngsters.

"But how can you live in such cold frozen places?" they ask.

"Oh, Hero and I live with my elders in warm igloos that we help build."

Studying lads on the playground, Khobi's eyes focus on a group of children fighting. He also thinks about his teachings: ACTIONS SPEAK LOUDER THAN WORDS.

"What's wrong with them?" Khobi asks, pointing to the scufflers.

"Oh," exclaimed Joey, "they're school bullies who always seem to be angry."

"Are they your friends?" asked Khobi.

"No," Susie hung her head showing sadness. "I don't fit in."

"Don't fit in! What does that mean?" Khobi was confused.

Linda and Hero are quickly becoming acquainted. Hero puts a smile on her face with his doggy licks.

Susie continues, " I'm not wanted in their group because I don't wear brand-name clothes. My parents don't make a lot of money. Their parents do!"

"I can never run fast enough," Joey adds.

"Some tell me I'm not pretty," Susie sobs.

"I live in a small house," Linda states humbly. "They live in mansions and buy all those video games stores sell. They're rich!"

"Rich!" Khobi wonders. "There are many ways to be rich, but I think our riches are different. Video games and brand-name clothes......I don't understand. Seems like all these riches called THINGS aren't bringing happiness...only unneeded clutter. They must have very sad hearts."

"Why do you think that?" asks Linda.

"Because they're acting mean to each other," answers Khobi with disapproval. "And Susie, I think you're very pretty!"

Susie's cheeks blush rosy red.

"I'm on my way to build an igloo to stay warm. I could use your help," invites the newcomer.

Together, Khobi, Hero and three ambitious peers find snow-covered ground outside the hustle and bustle of the city. A perfect site for an igloo, Khobi tells himself.

Joey, Linda, and Susie had never built a home made of snow to stay warm in and experienced so much fun doing work.

The snow is dense, glistening, and refreshing. Khobi knows the texture is perfect for making blocks. His elders have taught him well. He teaches the children the art of using their hands to pack the crystals together. The goods are put on a sled and Hero pulls the hefty load to the igloo site.

This hardy teammate is working too . . . . . . a sled dog *always* labors *eagerly* for his master.

The Arctic visitors' new residence is complete, just in time, before the light of day disappears.

Three children feel very good about themselves. They're exhausted, but experience a warm sensation they've never felt before.

Not really understanding what is happening inside of them (their hearts), the rookie igloo builders decide it's time to depart.

"Bye, Khobi," they all wave.

Hero wags his tail and Khobi swings his arms in the frosty air saying good-bye.

"Thank you for your help," he yells. "See how rich I am? I have three new friends!"

Happy faces went home with the threesome, putting a whole new meaning of "rich" into their hearts.

A deep smile garnishes Khobi's face creating a dimple in each cheek. Petting his nomadic partner, he reflects on their inseparable bond. Then his empty stomach interrupts with a rumble. "I'm starving! It's time to find something for us to eat."

Hero wags his tail and answers with his normal, "Whuff, Whuff, Whuuuuurrrrrrrrrrrrff. (I'm hungry too!)"

Nearby, a cold moving river flows with rapids under the ice cover. Khobi is an able fisherman. His elders taught him this valuable skill of survival. Patiently, he spears a delicious meal of fish for himself and his loyal Samoyed.

The scenery becomes a winter wonderland with snowflakes floating down from the cold air. Khobi sees his own breath when he speaks to his canine buddy. Ice crystals land on his face and Hero's fur. The glazed setting is a reminder of their beautiful Arctic homeland.

While these two appetites enjoy a feast, Hero's ears perk up straight as a pin. He whines softly. Khobi knows what Hero hears and smells is not danger. He also knows that his comrade can hear and smell what a master can't.

One instinctive protector gives a safe signal by wagging his tail, reporting everything is O.K.

He was right. A sled dog's senses far surpass that of man. Khobi never questions his guardian's intelligence.

The scent that Hero found and Khobi didn't was Joey, Linda, and Susie. They are greeted with wet friendly smooches from. . . . . . . Guess who?

"We would like to hear more about you and your dog," announces the fascinated trio.

"Really?" Khobi is thrilled to share his culture with his new friends.

Sitting around a campfire to stay warm, they quietly listen. Hero brushes his fur against everyone, absorbing hugs from each child. He can't be left out. That would be devastating for his spirit!

Khobi starts, "These beautiful dogs are Samoyeds. Their name comes from my nomadic people of the Samoyede tribe. In the earlier days my ancestors called them Bjelkiers. We are raised with these loving and gentle companions. They live with us and keep us warm in the cold frigid Arctic, way up North. Working is what they do best. Hero showed that when he helped build the igloo, pulling heavy loads of blocks stacked on a sled."

"How did both of you get here?" asks Joey.

"The whirling and swirling winds blew us here. Spirits of the elders knew we could bring happiness to unhappy children in your world," Khobi tells his circle of equals.

"Whuff, Whuff, Whuuuuurrrrrrrrrrrrrrrrrrrrrfff," agrees Hero.

Hearing this, Linda shares with sadness, "Sometimes I go home from school crying because others hurt me."

"Oh," Khobi sighs with compassion. "That must be their bad angry hearts at work."

"Really, what do you mean? I don't understand." Linda wants to hear more.

"My elders taught me to treat others like I want to be treated. They say angry hearts are not good and make you sad." Khobi explains, "the most skilled hunter in the village has a bad heart if he won't divide his catch with others who have less than him. When he shares his wealth, that is his good heart speaking."

And, Khobi adds, "all these THINGS children in your world have do not make them happy. Material things can't bring REAL happiness. That comes from your heart."

Joey listens. Connecting THINGS to happiness, he asks with curiosity, "Khobi, do you have THINGS?"

"I have all that I need," answers Khobi.

"You do?" Joey is surprised.

Khobi hugs Hero. "See this guy? He's my companion, protector, and best friend. Without him I can't survive. He keeps me warm on starry, cold nights and feels what I feel. When I hug him I become happy and strong, sharing love in return for his loyalty. Sometimes when sadness comes I remember what my elders have taught me. They believe you should be happy for what you do have, and not pout for what you don't have. I listen to them. They know best."

"Sounds like you're talking about respect." Linda is starting to understand.

"You're right. Do you respect your parents, teachers, and elders?" questions Khobi with directness.

"I'm really working on that. Guess we all need to," admits Linda.

"Does respect make a happy heart?" asks Susie.

"It sure does," confirms Khobi. "In my land we are taught very young to show respect to our elders. They teach us to do good, not bad; and tell us we're special, worth far more than any possession of our people. That's the best gift ever!"

"Khobi, you have such a happy heart. I want one like yours!" Susie is so excited.

"If I could give you mine I would. I can only share my happy feelings with you. Your heart can be filled with love and kindness, too! That's how Samoyede people feel inside."

Puzzled, Joey frowns. "Back to this THINGS stuff. When I get things, I'm happy for a short time."

"That's right, Joey", agrees Khobi. "Material things make you happy for a little while. Then those THINGS just seem to clutter your heart, taking away space for REAL happiness that comes from within. We share love and friendship in our daily lives. It makes us work harder and sleep better."

"I want to work harder and sleep better," repeats Joey.

"By helping build our igloo to stay warm, you did share your love and friendship. Do you feel different?" Khobi asks his friends.

Three smiles, six twinkling eyes, and hugs surrounding Hero give Khobi his answer.

After the children leave to go home for the second time, Khobi and Hero cuddle together. A thick plush Samoyed coat radiates heat, giving this compelling young statesman the warmth he needs for a good night's sleep.

"Hero, we must fill every child's heart with our kind of riches before the Arctic winds blow us home. Nuzzling his chilled frosty nose into a warm bundle of fur, Khobi realizes his mission is just beginning.

"We are RICH, Hero! So VERY RICH! Sweet dreams with ice crystals and snowflakes to our new world friends. We'll be here a while. They need us."

Khobi silently dozes off, cozy and content, with his arms wrapped around his best friend.

KHOBI & HERO

A CHILD'S HEART

a masterpiece unspoken
of what their life will be
touched by a world of confusion
with great indignities

this masterpiece so fragile
innocent of worldly ways
holds strength to cull the hurtings
that man portrays each day

this masterpiece unspoken
shares tenderness so real
a priceless resource given
to us, let it unveil

Susan D. Amundson

EPILOGUE

An agent of a seemingly lost culture wants to spread his powerful gift of love to all of our children. Although a culture itself may be dispelled, the cultural ways can be embedded through the greatest teacher, a child to a child.

Please come with Khobi and Hero on their journey of *A Child's Happy Heart.* There will be future Khobi and Hero books to tug at the core as these youngsters share themselves with you and your family.

ABOUT THE AUTHOR

Susan D. Amundson is inspired to write for children and their families through the heart of Khobi, descendant of the good-natured, loving Samoyede people who existed in ancient times.

Susan has worked with young children as an NREMT, Health Services, at Cooper Elementary School for eighteen years. She has lived with and studied Samoyeds for even longer. These two backgrounds come together in her creative writing of *A Child's Happy Heart.*

"Life was humble for my sister and I attending a one-room schoolhouse. More important, the frosting was secure confidence at home and at school. Children today live in a stressful changing time, but the basics of life taught then, remain as a solid foundation to all," states the author.

She resides in Hastings, MN with her husband of thirty years. They are parents of three grown successful children.

ABOUT THE ILLUSTRATOR

Brenda Joy Geiken has been drawing ever since childhood. In 1992, she graduated with an art degree from Northwestern College in St. Paul, Minnesota.

She has always desired to illustrate a children's book, and *A Child's Happy Heart* portrays her whimsical and innocent style.

"My family has always believed in me and has inspired me to be creative," states the illustrator. She thanks Susan D. Amundson for the opportunity to illustrate this heart–warming story.